A COLLECTION OF
MY FAVORITE RECIPES

THIS BOOK
BELONGS TO

....

....

....

For ordering customize book, please visit:

www.posondo.com/book

Table of Contents

NO	RECIPE NAME	PAGE

NO	RECIPE NAME	PAGE

NO	RECIPE NAME	PAGE

NO	RECIPE NAME	PAGE

No. | Recipe Name

Prep Time | Cook Time | Difficulty ○ ○ ○ ○ ○

Oven Temp | Date | Rating ☆ ☆ ☆ ☆ ☆

Serves 1 2 3 4 5 6 _ | Page

Ingredients

Directions

_____ _____

_____ _____

_____ _____

_____ _____

_____ _____

_____ _____

_____ _____

_____ _____

_____ _____

_____ _____

_____ _____

_____ _____

Personal Notes

_____

_____

_____

_____

_____

_____

_____

A yummu photo

No. | Recipe Name

Prep Time | Cook Time | Difficulty ○ ○ ○ ○ ○

Oven Temp | Date | Rating ☆ ☆ ☆ ☆ ☆

Serves 1 2 3 4 5 6 _ | Page

Ingredients

Directions

┌─ Personal Notes ─────────────────

A yummu photo

No.	Recipe Name

Prep Time	Cook Time	Difficulty ○ ○ ○ ○ ○
Oven Temp	Date	Rating ☆ ☆ ☆ ☆ ☆
Serves 1 2 3 4 5 6 _		Page

Ingredients

Directions

_____

_____

_____

_____

_____

_____

_____

_____

_____

_____

_____

_____

Personal Notes

A yummu photo

No.	Recipe Name

Prep Time	Cook Time	Difficulty ○ ○ ○ ○ ○
Oven Temp	Date	Rating ☆ ☆ ☆ ☆ ☆
Serves 1 2 3 4 5 6 _		Page

Ingredients   Directions

Personal Notes

A yummu photo

No.	Recipe Name

Prep Time	Cook Time	Difficulty ○ ○ ○ ○ ○
Oven Temp	Date	Rating ☆ ☆ ☆ ☆ ☆
Serves 1 2 3 4 5 6 _		Page

Ingredients   Directions

Personal Notes

A yummu photo

| No. | Recipe Name |

Prep Time	Cook Time	Difficulty ○ ○ ○ ○ ○
Oven Temp	Date	Rating ☆ ☆ ☆ ☆ ☆
Serves 1 2 3 4 5 6 _		Page

Ingredients

Directions

┌─ Personal Notes ──────────────

A yummu photo

No. | Recipe Name

Prep Time | Cook Time | Difficulty ○ ○ ○ ○ ○

Oven Temp | Date | Rating ☆ ☆ ☆ ☆ ☆

Serves 1 2 3 4 5 6 _ | Page

Ingredients

Directions

Personal Notes

A yummu photo

No. | Recipe Name

Prep Time | Cook Time | Difficulty ○ ○ ○ ○ ○

Oven Temp | Date | Rating ☆ ☆ ☆ ☆ ☆

Serves 1 2 3 4 5 6 _ | Page

Ingredients   Directions

Personal Notes

A yummu photo

No.	Recipe Name

Prep Time	Cook Time	Difficulty ○ ○ ○ ○ ○
Oven Temp	Date	Rating ☆ ☆ ☆ ☆ ☆
Serves 1 2 3 4 5 6 _		Page

Ingredients

Directions

_____ _____

_____ _____

_____ _____

_____ _____

_____ _____

_____ _____

_____ _____

_____ _____

_____ _____

_____ _____

_____ _____

_____ _____

_____ _____

_____ _____

_____ _____

┌ Personal Notes ─────────────────

A yummu photo

No.	Recipe Name

Prep Time	Cook Time	Difficulty ○ ○ ○ ○ ○

Oven Temp	Date	Rating ☆ ☆ ☆ ☆ ☆

Serves 1 2 3 4 5 6 _

Page

Ingredients

Directions

┌ Personal Notes ─────────────

A yummu photo

| No. | Recipe Name |

| Prep Time | Cook Time | Difficulty ○ ○ ○ ○ ○ |

| Oven Temp | Date | Rating ☆ ☆ ☆ ☆ ☆ |

| Serves 1 2 3 4 5 6 _ | Page |

Ingredients   Directions

_____   _____

_____   _____

_____   _____

_____   _____

_____   _____

_____   _____

_____   _____

_____   _____

_____   _____

_____   _____

_____   _____

_____   _____

┌ Personal Notes ─────────

_____

_____

_____

_____   A yummu photo

_____

_____

No. | Recipe Name

Prep Time | Cook Time | Difficulty ○ ○ ○ ○ ○

Oven Temp | Date | Rating ☆ ☆ ☆ ☆ ☆

Serves 1 2 3 4 5 6 _ | Page

Ingredients | Directions

Personal Notes

A yummu photo

No. | Recipe Name

Prep Time | Cook Time | Difficulty ○○○○○

Oven Temp | Date | Rating ☆☆☆☆☆

Serves 1 2 3 4 5 6 _ | Page

Ingredients   Directions

Personal Notes

A yummu photo

No. | Recipe Name

Prep Time | Cook Time | Difficulty ○○○○○

Oven Temp | Date | Rating ☆☆☆☆☆

Serves 1 2 3 4 5 6 _ | Page

Ingredients

Directions

┌─ Personal Notes ─────────────

A yummu photo

No. | Recipe Name

Prep Time | Cook Time | Difficulty ○ ○ ○ ○ ○

Oven Temp | Date | Rating ☆ ☆ ☆ ☆ ☆

Serves 1 2 3 4 5 6 _ | Page

Ingredients

Directions

Personal Notes

A yummu photo

No. | Recipe Name

Prep Time | Cook Time | Difficulty ○ ○ ○ ○ ○

Oven Temp | Date | Rating ☆ ☆ ☆ ☆ ☆

Serves 1 2 3 4 5 6 _ | Page

Ingredients   Directions

Personal Notes

A yummu photo

No. | Recipe Name

Prep Time | Cook Time | Difficulty ○ ○ ○ ○ ○

Oven Temp | Date | Rating ☆ ☆ ☆ ☆ ☆

Serves 1 2 3 4 5 6 _ | Page

Ingredients   Directions

Personal Notes

A yummu photo

No.   Recipe Name

Prep Time   Cook Time   Difficulty ○ ○ ○ ○ ○

Oven Temp   Date   Rating ☆ ☆ ☆ ☆ ☆

Serves 1 2 3 4 5 6 _   Page

Ingredients

Directions

Personal Notes

A yummu photo

No.	Recipe Name

Prep Time	Cook Time	Difficulty ○ ○ ○ ○ ○
Oven Temp	Date	Rating ☆ ☆ ☆ ☆ ☆

Serves 1 2 3 4 5 6 _

Page

Ingredients   Directions

Personal Notes

A yummu photo

No. | Recipe Name

Prep Time | Cook Time | Difficulty ○ ○ ○ ○ ○

Oven Temp | Date | Rating ☆ ☆ ☆ ☆ ☆

Serves 1 2 3 4 5 6 _ | Page

Ingredients | Directions

Personal Notes

A yummu photo

No. | Recipe Name

Prep Time | Cook Time | Difficulty ○ ○ ○ ○ ○

Oven Temp | Date | Rating ☆ ☆ ☆ ☆ ☆

Serves 1 2 3 4 5 6 _ | Page

Ingredients

Directions

┌─ Personal Notes ────────────────

A yummu photo

No. | Recipe Name

Prep Time | Cook Time | Difficulty ○ ○ ○ ○ ○

Oven Temp | Date | Rating ☆ ☆ ☆ ☆ ☆

Serves 1 2 3 4 5 6 _ | Page

Ingredients

Directions

Personal Notes

A yummu photo

No. | Recipe Name

Prep Time | Cook Time | Difficulty ○ ○ ○ ○ ○

Oven Temp | Date | Rating ☆ ☆ ☆ ☆ ☆

Serves 1 2 3 4 5 6 _ | Page

Ingredients | Directions

Personal Notes

A yummu photo

No.	Recipe Name

Prep Time	Cook Time	Difficulty ○ ○ ○ ○ ○
Oven Temp	Date	Rating ☆ ☆ ☆ ☆ ☆
Serves 1 2 3 4 5 6 _		Page

Ingredients   Directions

_____   _____

_____   _____

_____   _____

_____   _____

_____   _____

_____   _____

_____   _____

_____   _____

_____   _____

_____   _____

_____   _____

_____   _____

┌ Personal Notes ──────────────

_____

_____

_____

_____

_____

_____

_____

A yummu photo

| No. | Recipe Name |

| Prep Time | Cook Time | Difficulty ○ ○ ○ ○ ○ |

| Oven Temp | Date | Rating ☆ ☆ ☆ ☆ ☆ |

| Serves 1 2 3 4 5 6 _ | Page |

Ingredients

Directions

┌ Personal Notes ──────────

A yummu photo

No. | Recipe Name

Prep Time | Cook Time | Difficulty ○ ○ ○ ○ ○

Oven Temp | Date | Rating ☆ ☆ ☆ ☆ ☆

Serves 1 2 3 4 5 6 _ | Page

Ingredients   Directions

Personal Notes

A yummu photo

No. | Recipe Name

Prep Time | Cook Time | Difficulty ○ ○ ○ ○ ○

Oven Temp | Date | Rating ☆ ☆ ☆ ☆ ☆

Serves 1 2 3 4 5 6 _ | Page

Ingredients | ## Directions

Personal Notes

A yummu photo

No. Recipe Name

Prep Time Cook Time Difficulty ◯ ◯ ◯ ◯ ◯

Oven Temp Date Rating ☆ ☆ ☆ ☆ ☆

Serves 1 2 3 4 5 6 _ Page

Ingredients Directions

Personal Notes

A yummu photo

No.	Recipe Name

Prep Time	Cook Time	Difficulty ○ ○ ○ ○ ○
Oven Temp	Date	Rating ☆ ☆ ☆ ☆ ☆
Serves 1 2 3 4 5 6 _		Page

Ingredients   Directions

Personal Notes

A yummu photo

No.   Recipe Name

Prep Time   Cook Time   Difficulty ○ ○ ○ ○ ○

Oven Temp   Date   Rating   ☆ ☆ ☆ ☆ ☆

Serves 1 2 3 4 5 6 _   Page

Ingredients   Directions

Personal Notes

A yummu photo

No.	Recipe Name

Prep Time	Cook Time	Difficulty ○ ○ ○ ○ ○
Oven Temp	Date	Rating ☆ ☆ ☆ ☆ ☆
Serves 1 2 3 4 5 6 _		Page

Ingredients   Directions

_____   _____

_____   _____

_____   _____

_____   _____

_____   _____

_____   _____

_____   _____

_____   _____

_____   _____

_____   _____

_____   _____

_____   _____

┌ Personal Notes ─────────────

_____

_____

_____

_____

_____

_____

A yummu photo

No. | Recipe Name

Prep Time | Cook Time | Difficulty ○ ○ ○ ○ ○

Oven Temp | Date | Rating ☆ ☆ ☆ ☆ ☆

Serves 1 2 3 4 5 6 _ | Page

Ingredients   Directions

Personal Notes

A yummu photo

No. | Recipe Name

Prep Time | Cook Time | Difficulty ◯ ◯ ◯ ◯ ◯

Oven Temp | Date | Rating ☆ ☆ ☆ ☆ ☆

Serves 1 2 3 4 5 6 _ | Page

Ingredients

Directions

┌ Personal Notes ─────────────

A yummu photo

No. | Recipe Name

Prep Time | Cook Time | Difficulty ○ ○ ○ ○ ○

Oven Temp | Date | Rating ☆ ☆ ☆ ☆ ☆

Serves 1 2 3 4 5 6 _ | Page

Ingredients   Directions

Personal Notes

A yummu photo

No.	Recipe Name

Prep Time	Cook Time	Difficulty ○ ○ ○ ○ ○
Oven Temp	Date	Rating ☆ ☆ ☆ ☆ ☆
Serves 1 2 3 4 5 6 _		Page

Ingredients   Directions

_____   _____

_____   _____

_____   _____

_____   _____

_____   _____

_____   _____

_____   _____

_____   _____

_____   _____

_____   _____

_____   _____

_____   _____

Personal Notes

_____

_____

_____

_____   A yummu photo

_____

_____

_____

No.	Recipe Name

Prep Time	Cook Time	Difficulty ○ ○ ○ ○ ○
Oven Temp	Date	Rating ☆ ☆ ☆ ☆ ☆
Serves 1 2 3 4 5 6 _		Page

Ingredients   Directions

Personal Notes

A yummu photo

No. | Recipe Name

Prep Time | Cook Time | Difficulty ○ ○ ○ ○ ○

Oven Temp | Date | Rating ☆ ☆ ☆ ☆ ☆

Serves 1 2 3 4 5 6 _ | Page

Ingredients | Directions

┌ Personal Notes ─────────────

A yummu photo

No. | Recipe Name

Prep Time | Cook Time | Difficulty ○ ○ ○ ○ ○

Oven Temp | Date | Rating ☆ ☆ ☆ ☆ ☆

Serves 1 2 3 4 5 6 _ | Page

Ingredients   Directions

Personal Notes

A yummu photo

No.	Recipe Name

Prep Time	Cook Time	Difficulty ○ ○ ○ ○ ○
Oven Temp	Date	Rating ☆ ☆ ☆ ☆ ☆
Serves 1 2 3 4 5 6 _		Page

Ingredients

Directions

_____ _____

_____ _____

_____ _____

_____ _____

_____ _____

_____ _____

_____ _____

_____ _____

_____ _____

_____ _____

_____ _____

_____ _____

┌ Personal Notes ──────────────

_____

_____

_____

_____   A yummu photo

_____

_____

_____

No.	Recipe Name

Prep Time	Cook Time	Difficulty ○ ○ ○ ○ ○
Oven Temp	Date	Rating ☆ ☆ ☆ ☆ ☆
Serves 1 2 3 4 5 6 _		Page

Ingredients   Directions

_____   _____

_____   _____

_____   _____

_____   _____

_____   _____

_____   _____

_____   _____

_____   _____

_____   _____

_____   _____

_____   _____

_____   _____

_____   _____

┌─ Personal Notes ───────────────

A yummu photo

No. | Recipe Name
_____

Prep Time | Cook Time | Difficulty ○ ○ ○ ○ ○

Oven Temp | Date | Rating ☆ ☆ ☆ ☆ ☆

Serves 1 2 3 4 5 6 _ | Page

Ingredients

_____
_____
_____
_____
_____
_____
_____
_____
_____
_____
_____
_____
_____

Directions

_____
_____
_____
_____
_____
_____
_____
_____
_____
_____
_____
_____
_____

Personal Notes

_____
_____
_____
_____
_____
_____
_____

A yummu photo

No.	Recipe Name

Prep Time	Cook Time	Difficulty ○ ○ ○ ○ ○
Oven Temp	Date	Rating ☆ ☆ ☆ ☆ ☆

Serves 1 2 3 4 5 6 _

Page

Ingredients   Directions

Personal Notes

A yummu photo

No. | Recipe Name

Prep Time | Cook Time | Difficulty ○ ○ ○ ○ ○

Oven Temp | Date | Rating ☆ ☆ ☆ ☆ ☆

Serves 1 2 3 4 5 6 _ | Page

Ingredients

Directions

─ Personal Notes ─────────

A yummu photo

No. | Recipe Name

Prep Time | Cook Time | Difficulty ○ ○ ○ ○ ○

Oven Temp | Date | Rating ☆ ☆ ☆ ☆ ☆

Serves 1 2 3 4 5 6 _ | Page

Ingredients   Directions

Personal Notes

A yummu photo

| No. | Recipe Name |

| Prep Time | Cook Time | Difficulty ○ ○ ○ ○ ○ |

| Oven Temp | Date | Rating ☆ ☆ ☆ ☆ ☆ |

| Serves 1 2 3 4 5 6 _ | Page |

Ingredients   Directions

Personal Notes

A yummu photo

No. | Recipe Name

Prep Time | Cook Time | Difficulty ○ ○ ○ ○ ○

Oven Temp | Date | Rating ☆ ☆ ☆ ☆ ☆

Serves 1 2 3 4 5 6 _ | Page

Ingredients   Directions

Personal Notes

A yummu photo

No.	Recipe Name

Prep Time	Cook Time	Difficulty ○ ○ ○ ○ ○
Oven Temp	Date	Rating ☆ ☆ ☆ ☆ ☆
Serves 1 2 3 4 5 6 _		Page

Ingredients   Directions

Personal Notes

A yummu photo

No. | Recipe Name

Prep Time | Cook Time | Difficulty ○ ○ ○ ○ ○

Oven Temp | Date | Rating ☆ ☆ ☆ ☆ ☆

Serves 1 2 3 4 5 6 _ | Page

Ingredients

Directions

┌─ Personal Notes ─────────────

A yummu photo

No. | Recipe Name

Prep Time | Cook Time | Difficulty ○ ○ ○ ○ ○

Oven Temp | Date | Rating ☆ ☆ ☆ ☆ ☆

Serves 1 2 3 4 5 6 _ | Page

Ingredients

Directions

┌ Personal Notes ─────────────

A yummu photo

No.	Recipe Name

Prep Time	Cook Time	Difficulty ○ ○ ○ ○ ○
Oven Temp	Date	Rating ☆ ☆ ☆ ☆ ☆
Serves 1 2 3 4 5 6 _		Page

Ingredients   Directions

Personal Notes

A yummu photo

No. | Recipe Name

Prep Time | Cook Time | Difficulty ○ ○ ○ ○ ○

Oven Temp | Date | Rating ☆ ☆ ☆ ☆ ☆

Serves 1 2 3 4 5 6 _ | Page

Ingredients

Directions

_____

_____

_____

_____

_____

_____

_____

_____

_____

_____

_____

┌ Personal Notes ─────────

A yummu photo

No. | Recipe Name

Prep Time | Cook Time | Difficulty ○ ○ ○ ○ ○

Oven Temp | Date | Rating ☆ ☆ ☆ ☆ ☆

Serves 1 2 3 4 5 6 _ | Page

Ingredients | Directions

Personal Notes

A yummu photo

No. | Recipe Name

Prep Time | Cook Time | Difficulty ○ ○ ○ ○ ○

Oven Temp | Date | Rating ☆ ☆ ☆ ☆ ☆

Serves 1 2 3 4 5 6 _ | Page

Ingredients   Directions

r Personal Notes

A yummu photo

No.	Recipe Name

Prep Time	Cook Time	Difficulty ○ ○ ○ ○ ○
Oven Temp	Date	Rating ☆ ☆ ☆ ☆ ☆

Serves 1 2 3 4 5 6 _

Page

Ingredients

Directions

Personal Notes

A yummu photo

No.	Recipe Name

Prep Time	Cook Time	Difficulty ○ ○ ○ ○ ○
Oven Temp	Date	Rating ☆ ☆ ☆ ☆ ☆
Serves 1 2 3 4 5 6 _		Page

Ingredients   Directions

Personal Notes

A yummu photo

No.	Recipe Name

Prep Time	Cook Time	Difficulty ○ ○ ○ ○ ○
Oven Temp	Date	Rating ☆ ☆ ☆ ☆ ☆
Serves 1 2 3 4 5 6 _		Page

Ingredients   Directions

_____   _____
_____   _____
_____   _____
_____   _____
_____   _____
_____   _____
_____   _____
_____   _____
_____   _____
_____   _____
_____   _____
_____   _____
_____   _____

┌ Personal Notes ─────────────────
_____
_____
_____
_____
_____
_____
_____

A yummu photo

No. | Recipe Name

Prep Time | Cook Time | Difficulty ○ ○ ○ ○ ○

Oven Temp | Date | Rating ☆ ☆ ☆ ☆ ☆

Serves 1 2 3 4 5 6 _ | Page

Ingredients

Directions

┌ Personal Notes ─────────────

A yummu photo

No. | Recipe Name

Prep Time | Cook Time | Difficulty ○ ○ ○ ○ ○

Oven Temp | Date | Rating ☆ ☆ ☆ ☆ ☆

Serves 1 2 3 4 5 6 _ | Page

Ingredients | Directions

Personal Notes

A yummu photo

No.	Recipe Name

Prep Time	Cook Time	Difficulty ○ ○ ○ ○ ○
Oven Temp	Date	Rating ☆ ☆ ☆ ☆ ☆
Serves 1 2 3 4 5 6 _		Page

Ingredients   Directions

Personal Notes

A yummu photo

No. | Recipe Name

Prep Time | Cook Time | Difficulty ○ ○ ○ ○ ○

Oven Temp | Date | Rating ☆ ☆ ☆ ☆ ☆

Serves 1 2 3 4 5 6 _ | Page

Ingredients

Directions

Personal Notes

A yummu photo

No. | Recipe Name

Prep Time | Cook Time | Difficulty ○ ○ ○ ○ ○

Oven Temp | Date | Rating ☆ ☆ ☆ ☆ ☆

Serves 1 2 3 4 5 6 _ | Page

Ingredients

Directions

┌ Personal Notes ─────────────

A yummu photo

No.	Recipe Name

Prep Time	Cook Time	Difficulty ○ ○ ○ ○ ○
Oven Temp	Date	Rating ☆ ☆ ☆ ☆ ☆
Serves 1 2 3 4 5 6 _		Page

Ingredients   Directions

Personal Notes

A yummu photo

No. | Recipe Name

Prep Time | Cook Time | Difficulty ○ ○ ○ ○ ○

Oven Temp | Date | Rating ☆ ☆ ☆ ☆ ☆

Serves 1 2 3 4 5 6 _ | Page

Ingredients

Directions

Personal Notes

A yummu photo

No.	Recipe Name

Prep Time	Cook Time	Difficulty ○ ○ ○ ○ ○
Oven Temp	Date	Rating ☆ ☆ ☆ ☆ ☆
Serves 1 2 3 4 5 6 _		Page

Ingredients

Directions

Personal Notes

A yummu photo

No. | Recipe Name

Prep Time | Cook Time | Difficulty ○ ○ ○ ○ ○

Oven Temp | Date | Rating ☆ ☆ ☆ ☆ ☆

Serves 1 2 3 4 5 6 _ | Page

Ingredients

Directions

┌ Personal Notes ─────────

A yummu photo

No. | Recipe Name

Prep Time | Cook Time | Difficulty ○ ○ ○ ○ ○

Oven Temp | Date | Rating ☆ ☆ ☆ ☆ ☆

Serves 1 2 3 4 5 6 _ | Page

Ingredients

Directions

Personal Notes

A yummu photo

No. | Recipe Name

Prep Time | Cook Time | Difficulty ○ ○ ○ ○ ○

Oven Temp | Date | Rating ☆ ☆ ☆ ☆ ☆

Serves 1 2 3 4 5 6 _ | Page

Ingredients   Directions

_____   _____

_____   _____

_____   _____

_____   _____

_____   _____

_____   _____

_____   _____

_____   _____

_____   _____

_____   _____

_____   _____

_____   _____

_____

Personal Notes

_____

_____

_____

_____   A yummu photo

_____

_____

_____

No.	Recipe Name

Prep Time	Cook Time	Difficulty ○ ○ ○ ○ ○

Oven Temp	Date	Rating ☆ ☆ ☆ ☆ ☆

Serves 1 2 3 4 5 6 _

Page

Ingredients   Directions

Personal Notes

A yummu photo

No. | Recipe Name

Prep Time | Cook Time | Difficulty ○ ○ ○ ○ ○

Oven Temp | Date | Rating ☆ ☆ ☆ ☆ ☆

Serves 1 2 3 4 5 6 _ | Page

Ingredients | Directions

Personal Notes

A yummu photo

No. | Recipe Name

Prep Time | Cook Time | Difficulty ○ ○ ○ ○ ○

Oven Temp | Date | Rating ☆ ☆ ☆ ☆ ☆

Serves 1 2 3 4 5 6 _ | Page

Ingredients | Directions

Personal Notes

A yummu photo

No. | Recipe Name

Prep Time | Cook Time | Difficulty ○ ○ ○ ○ ○

Oven Temp | Date | Rating ☆ ☆ ☆ ☆ ☆

Serves 1 2 3 4 5 6 _ | Page

Ingredients

Directions

Personal Notes

A yummu photo

No. | Recipe Name

Prep Time | Cook Time | Difficulty ○ ○ ○ ○ ○

Oven Temp | Date | Rating ☆ ☆ ☆ ☆ ☆

Serves 1 2 3 4 5 6 _ | Page

Ingredients   Directions

Personal Notes

A yummu photo

No. | Recipe Name

Prep Time | Cook Time | Difficulty ○ ○ ○ ○ ○

Oven Temp | Date | Rating ☆ ☆ ☆ ☆ ☆

Serves 1 2 3 4 5 6 _ | Page

Ingredients | Directions

------- | ------------------------------

------- | ------------------------------

------- | ------------------------------

------- | ------------------------------

------- | ------------------------------

------- | ------------------------------

------- | ------------------------------

------- | ------------------------------

------- | ------------------------------

------- | ------------------------------

------- | ------------------------------

------- | ------------------------------

------- | ------------------------------

┌ Personal Notes ────────────

A yummu photo

No. | Recipe Name

Prep Time | Cook Time | Difficulty ○ ○ ○ ○ ○

Oven Temp | Date | Rating ☆ ☆ ☆ ☆ ☆

Serves 1 2 3 4 5 6 _ | Page

Ingredients

Directions

┌─ Personal Notes ─────────

A yummu photo

No. | Recipe Name

Prep Time | Cook Time | Difficulty ○ ○ ○ ○ ○

Oven Temp | Date | Rating ☆ ☆ ☆ ☆ ☆

Serves 1 2 3 4 5 6 _ | Page

Ingredients

Directions

┌ Personal Notes ─────────────

A yummu photo

No. | Recipe Name

Prep Time | Cook Time | Difficulty ○ ○ ○ ○ ○

Oven Temp | Date | Rating ☆ ☆ ☆ ☆ ☆

Serves 1 2 3 4 5 6 _ | Page

Ingredients

Directions

Personal Notes

A yummu photo

No.	Recipe Name

Prep Time | Cook Time | Difficulty ○ ○ ○ ○ ○

Oven Temp | Date | Rating ☆ ☆ ☆ ☆ ☆

Serves 1 2 3 4 5 6 _ | Page

Ingredients   Directions

_____   _____
_____   _____
_____   _____
_____   _____
_____   _____
_____   _____
_____   _____
_____   _____
_____   _____
_____   _____
_____   _____
_____   _____
_____   _____

┌ Personal Notes ─────────

A yummu photo

No. | Recipe Name

Prep Time | Cook Time | Difficulty ○ ○ ○ ○ ○

Oven Temp | Date | Rating ☆ ☆ ☆ ☆ ☆

Serves 1 2 3 4 5 6 _ | Page

Ingredients   Directions

Personal Notes

A yummu photo

| No. | Recipe Name |

| Prep Time | Cook Time | Difficulty ○ ○ ○ ○ ○ |

| Oven Temp | Date | Rating ☆ ☆ ☆ ☆ ☆ |

| Serves 1 2 3 4 5 6 _ | Page |

Ingredients   Directions

_____   _____

_____   _____

_____   _____

_____   _____

_____   _____

_____   _____

_____   _____

_____   _____

_____   _____

_____   _____

_____   _____

_____   _____

_____   _____

Personal Notes

_____

_____

_____

_____   A yummu photo

_____

_____

No. | Recipe Name _____

Prep Time | Cook Time | Difficulty ○ ○ ○ ○ ○

Oven Temp | Date | Rating ☆ ☆ ☆ ☆ ☆

Serves 1 2 3 4 5 6 _ | Page

Ingredients

Directions

_____ _____
_____ _____
_____ _____
_____ _____
_____ _____
_____ _____
_____ _____
_____ _____
_____ _____
_____ _____
_____ _____
_____ _____
_____ _____

Personal Notes
_____
_____
_____
_____
_____
_____
_____

A yummu photo

No.	Recipe Name

Prep Time	Cook Time	Difficulty ○ ○ ○ ○ ○
Oven Temp	Date	Rating ☆ ☆ ☆ ☆ ☆
Serves 1 2 3 4 5 6 _		Page

Ingredients   Directions

_____   _____

_____   _____

_____   _____

_____   _____

_____   _____

_____   _____

_____   _____

_____   _____

_____   _____

_____   _____

_____   _____

_____   _____

_____   _____

┌ Personal Notes ─────────────

A yummu photo

No. | Recipe Name

Prep Time | Cook Time | Difficulty ○ ○ ○ ○ ○

Oven Temp | Date | Rating ☆ ☆ ☆ ☆ ☆

Serves 1 2 3 4 5 6 _ | Page

Ingredients

Directions

Personal Notes

A yummu photo

No.	Recipe Name

Prep Time	Cook Time	Difficulty ○ ○ ○ ○ ○
Oven Temp	Date	Rating ☆ ☆ ☆ ☆ ☆
Serves 1 2 3 4 5 6 _		Page

Ingredients   Directions

_____   _____
_____   _____
_____   _____
_____   _____
_____   _____
_____   _____
_____   _____
_____   _____
_____   _____
_____   _____
_____   _____
_____   _____

Personal Notes
_____
_____
_____
_____
_____
_____
_____

A yummu photo

No.	Recipe Name

Prep Time	Cook Time	Difficulty ○ ○ ○ ○ ○
Oven Temp	Date	Rating ☆ ☆ ☆ ☆ ☆
Serves 1 2 3 4 5 6 _		Page

Ingredients   Directions

_____   _____
_____   _____
_____   _____
_____   _____
_____   _____
_____   _____
_____   _____
_____   _____
_____   _____
_____   _____
_____   _____
_____   _____
_____   _____

┌ Personal Notes ─────────────

A yummu photo

No. | Recipe Name

Prep Time | Cook Time | Difficulty ○ ○ ○ ○ ○

Oven Temp | Date | Rating ☆ ☆ ☆ ☆ ☆

Serves 1 2 3 4 5 6 _ | Page

Ingredients | Directions

Personal Notes

A yummu photo

No. Recipe Name

Prep Time | Cook Time | Difficulty ○ ○ ○ ○ ○

Oven Temp | Date | Rating ☆ ☆ ☆ ☆ ☆

Serves 1 2 3 4 5 6 _ | Page

Ingredients   Directions

┌ Personal Notes ─────────────

A yummu photo

No. | Recipe Name

Prep Time | Cook Time | Difficulty ○ ○ ○ ○ ○

Oven Temp | Date | Rating ☆ ☆ ☆ ☆ ☆

Serves 1 2 3 4 5 6 _ | Page

Ingredients

Directions

Personal Notes

A yummu photo

No. | Recipe Name
_____

Prep Time | Cook Time | Difficulty ○ ○ ○ ○ ○

Oven Temp | Date | Rating ☆ ☆ ☆ ☆ ☆

Serves 1 2 3 4 5 6 _ | Page

Ingredients   Directions

_____ _____

_____ _____

_____ _____

_____ _____

_____ _____

_____ _____

_____ _____

_____ _____

_____ _____

_____ _____

_____ _____

_____ _____

_____ _____

Personal Notes

_____

_____

_____

_____

_____

_____

_____

A yummu photo

No. Recipe Name

Prep Time | Cook Time | Difficulty ○ ○ ○ ○ ○

Oven Temp | Date | Rating ☆ ☆ ☆ ☆ ☆

Serves 1 2 3 4 5 6 _ | Page

Ingredients

Directions

Personal Notes

A yummu photo

No. | Recipe Name

Prep Time | Cook Time | Difficulty ○ ○ ○ ○ ○

Oven Temp | Date | Rating ☆ ☆ ☆ ☆ ☆

Serves 1 2 3 4 5 6 _ | Page

Ingredients | Directions

Personal Notes

A yummu photo

No. | Recipe Name

Prep Time | Cook Time | Difficulty ○ ○ ○ ○ ○

Oven Temp | Date | Rating ☆ ☆ ☆ ☆ ☆

Serves 1 2 3 4 5 6 _ | Page

Ingredients   Directions

_____ _____

_____ _____

_____ _____

_____ _____

_____ _____

_____ _____

_____ _____

_____ _____

_____ _____

_____ _____

_____ _____

_____ _____

_____ _____

┌ Personal Notes ─────────────

A yummu photo

No. | Recipe Name

Prep Time | Cook Time | Difficulty ○ ○ ○ ○ ○

Oven Temp | Date | Rating ☆ ☆ ☆ ☆ ☆

Serves 1 2 3 4 5 6 _ | Page

Ingredients   Directions

_____ _____

_____ _____

_____ _____

_____ _____

_____ _____

_____ _____

_____ _____

_____ _____

_____ _____

_____ _____

_____ _____

_____

Personal Notes

_____

_____

_____

_____

_____

_____

_____

A yummu photo

For ordering customize book, please visit:

www.posondo.com/book

Made in the USA
Monee, IL
09 January 2023

24831694R00057